HOW TO RUN

THE AMAZING
R A C E

FOR CAMPS AND YOUTH CENTERS

CURT JACKSON

HOW TO RUN THE AMAZING RACE
FOR CAMPS YOUTH CENTERS
By Curt Jackson
Copyright © 2019
Moosehead Publishing, Florida

All Rights Reserved. No part of this publication may be reproduced or distributed in any form or by any means, electronic or mechanical, including photocopying and recording, without express permission of the author.

Brief quotations may be used in reviews prepared for inclusion in a magazine, newspaper, or for broadcast.

This book has not been prepared, approved or licensed by any entity that created or produced the television show The Amazing Race.

ISBN: 9781079956771
Imprint: Independently published

Cover Design: Curt Jackson
To contact author, email curt@recreationpros.com.

TABLE OF CONTENTS

INTRO 6
BASICS OF THE AMAZING RACE 8
SETTING UP YOUR AMAZING RACE 14
PLANNING CHECKLIST 20
IN-CAMP EXAMPLE (2-3 HOURS) 24
    DISCUSSION OF RULES 25
    PRE-RACE ANNOUNCEMENT 26
    THE RACE 28
IN-CAMP CHALLENGES 32
  GENERAL CHALLENGES 34
    TOASTED MALLOWS 35
    IT'S PUZZLING 36
    LEADING THE BLIND 37
    ALL FOR ONE 39
    WHERE THERE'S A WILL 40
    SHOW ME SOME ID 41
    SOME ASSEMBLY REQUIRED 42
    SCAVENGING FOR NATURE 43
    CAN YOU HACK IT? 44
    BEANS IN A JAR 45
    FROZEN 46
    IT'S FREE TO THROW 47
    ABRACADABRA 48
    HUNT EGGSTRAVAGANZA 49
    ALL WRAPPED UP 50
    PUTT IT THERE, MY FIREND 51
    ALL TIED UP 52
    CHARADES 53
    SHIP BUILDERS 54
    TALK TO THE HAND 55
    DO YOU REMEMBER? 56
  ROADBLOCKS 58
    A BIRD'S PARADISE 59
    YOUR NUMBER'S UP 60
    1982 61
    HEADS UP 62
    FLAGS AHOY 63

    IT'S A TOSS UP 64
    HAWKEYE 65
    CARD NINJA 66
    ZIP IT 67
    RING-A-DING 68
    GOO GOO 69
    A BUG'S LIFE 70
    MARSHMALLOW ATTACK 71
    YOU SPIN ME RIGHT ROUND 72
DETOURS 74
    BRAINS OR BRAWN? 75
    PACK IT OR STACK IT? 76
    TIE IT OR FIND IT? 77
    DOG OR CAT? 78
    HACK OR HUNT? 79
INTERSECTIONS 80
    HUMAN ALPHABET 81
    TELEPHONE FACE TIME 82
    TEAM JIGSAW 83
    WATER BALLOON TOSS 84

VARIATIONS 86
    AROUND THE WORLD 86
    OFF-SITE 90
    OFF-SITE WITH PHOTOS 94
    TIME TRAVEL 98
    COLOR WAR STYLE 100
    OTHER VARIATIONS 104

SUGGESTED ADDITIONS 106
    TRANSPORTATION HUBS and TOKENS 107
    USING DICE (WAS THERE A DELAY?) 108
    SWITCH PASSES 109
    HIDDEN EXPRESS PASS 110
    TRAVELING GNOMES 111
    PENALTY FOR NEGATIVE BEHAVIOR OR CHEATING 112

TEMPLATES 117

ABOUT THE AUTHOR 114

INTRO

The Amazing Race is a reality television competition where teams of two people race around the world completing tasks. There are usually 12 legs of the race, with each leg ending in a "Pit Stop". On each episode, there is usually one team that is eliminated for getting to the Pit Stop (the end of that leg of the race) last. But you probably know all of this, because The Amazing Race is a worldwide phenomenon.

It has also been the theme of a lot of birthday parties, adult scavenger hunts and summer camp programs. As anyone who has put together an Amazing Race party or event knows, it's not easy to pull it off. It takes a lot of planning to do it right. **This book is meant to make the planning process much easier and help make your event a total success.**

The first time I planned an Amazing Race program was for a summer camp for middle school aged kids. Each group was chaperoned by a staff member or two and the teams raced around San Diego using their feet and the city transit system. It took a good amount of work to set up the one-day competition. It involved planning the route, contacting businesses that we wanted the teams to visit (restaurants, hotels, a variety of shops, a movie theater, and a police department), making the clues and envelopes, deciding on how much we needed for the transit, and more.

There were some hiccups, but overall the kids and staff had a great time, despite being exhausted at the end of the day. I learned a lot from that first experience.

Since then, I have put together other Amazing Races for camps and have spoken with many camp and recreation professionals who have done their own Amazing Races. In my research for new and improved ways of tweaking my own programs, **I have come across some brilliant ideas, variations and warnings that I'll share with you** as well.

Are you ready to plan your own Amazing race? Then, let's get started. (You did say "yes", right?)

PLEASE NOTE: While this book was written for youth and camp leaders, all of the information can be used for an adult event as well.

BASICS OF THE AMAZING RACE

In the television show, teams race around the world via airplanes, taxis, walking/running, and other, more unique, modes of transportation. Your race will be probably all be on foot. However, if you take the race off-site, you can incorporate different modes of transportation like busses, trams, etc.

Along the way, teams receive envelopes from clue boxes, after they complete a task, and at the beginning of a leg. These envelopes usually contain instructions for a task the team must complete, or they can contain Route Info, Detours, Roadblocks and more.

During the race teams must complete a series of tasks/challenges during the race. **The tasks can be just about anything, construction related, skill related, memory related, fear related, eating, etc.** In this book I have provided a number of challenges to use for your Amazing Race.

Let's take a look at the Route Markers and the different cards teams will come across.

At the end of this book is a web address where I provide downloadable templates for each of these cards for you to use. Yes, they are in color.

ROUTE MARKERS

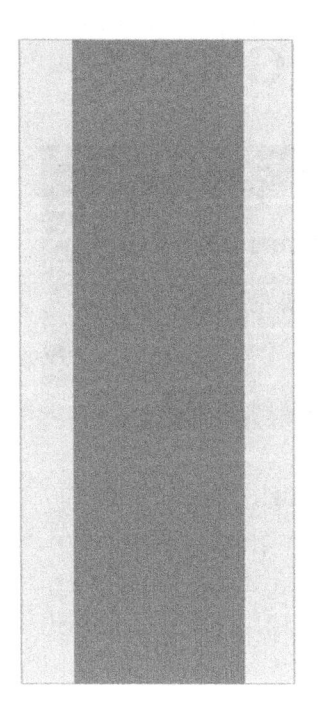

Route Markers are red and yellow colored flags that mark where the teams must go. They can be on clue boxes, attached to buildings to show where to go, or even along a path.

ROUTE INFO

This card tells teams where to go next. It gives the location, but teams must figure out how to get there. It also may give instructions on how teams must travel (by plane, by foot, etc.). The destination may be given in a cryptic manner.

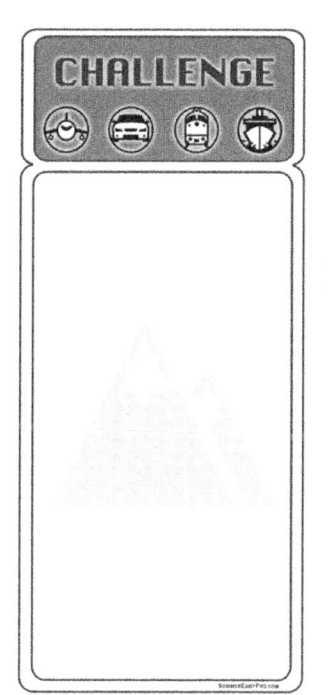

CHALLENGE CARDS

A challenge card contains instructions for a task that must be completed before moving on. These are usually in a clue box that is located in front of the area the task takes place.

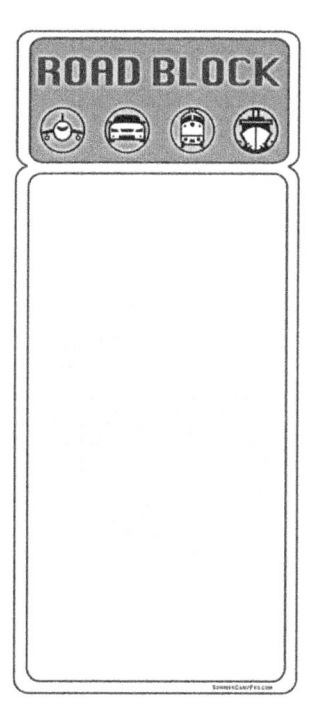

ROAD BLOCKS

This is a task that only one member of the team can complete. The other person can usually give encouragement or advice, but they cannot physically help. Players must take turns performing the Road Blocks. In other words, teams cannot have the same person complete all the Road Blocks.

For your event, each team will probably have more than two people, so a Road Block, in this instance, could be a task that only one OR two players would complete, but not the whole team.

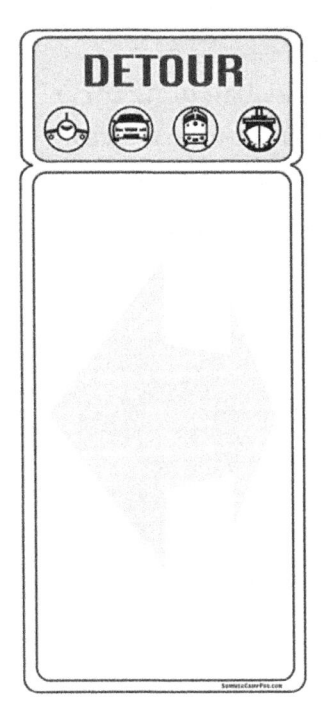

DETOURS

This is a choice of two tasks. Teams may choose between the tasks and can switch tasks at any time. Teams only need to complete one of them successfully.

INTERSECTION

This is a task where two teams must work together to accomplish it. Teams can choose which other team they want to work with, which means they might be able to start on the task right away, or they may decide to wait for a team they have an alliance with, but that could be a long wait.

OTHER CARDS

There are other cards in the show, like Yields, U-Turns, Fast Forwards, and more, but **I don't like the idea of teams being able to penalize others or being able to jump to first place simply by completing one task**, especially when the teams are made up of young players. So, I'm leaving those out.

NO ELIMINATIONS

At the end of a leg (around 11 or 12 tasks), one team is usually eliminated. For our purposes, **we will not be eliminating any teams**. Besides, I am guessing that most event planners reading this will not want to create more than 1 leg (12 tasks) for the whole race.

The first team to arrive at the final Pit Stop, wins.

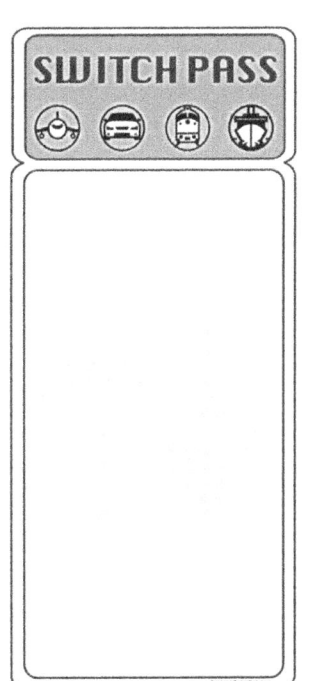

SUGGESTED ADDITIONS

I have included additions specifically for a youth Amazing Race in the Suggested Additions section at the end of the book. The inclusion of Transportation Hubs, Tokens, Switch Passes, etc. can add a lot of excitement to the race.

SETTING UP YOUR AMAZING RACE

There is a lot that goes into setting up an Amazing Race. Don't get overwhelmed, though. Planning and creating the event should be a fun part of the process.

Once you are done with the planning, it's time to actually set-up the equipment, decorations, etc. for the race. This should also be enjoyable. Just make sure you **give yourself and your team plenty of time to do everything**. Don't add stress to your life by doing everything last minute. And make sure to delegate as much as possible.

In this section we'll go over things you need to think about during your planning. I've included a couple of checklists.

HOW LONG WILL THE RACE BE?
Begin by determining how long the race will run. Will it be a two-hour program, a day long race, or will you extend it throughout the week by doing a couple of hours each day?

While I have put together day long races, I prefer shorter ones, maybe half-day. A week-long race might be similar to a traditional, overnight camp color war program. It's all up to you and what you think would work for your program.

WILL THE RACE TAKE PLACE ON-SITE OR WILL IT BE OFF-SITE?
Running an Amazing Race program on-site is much easier than one that takes teams off-site. However, there is an added sense of excitement when campers get to leave the property. Still, if I were to take the race off-site with youth it would only be with teens, and it would need to be an all-day program.

WILL IT BE THEMED?
I don't think an Amazing Race needs to be themed (except for maybe an Around the World theme – especially if you have international staff). You'll have enough to focus on without the added theme details. That said, if you want to add a theme, you certainly can, especially if you have a few races under your belt and the general planning has already been created. Check out the Variations section on page 79 for ideas.

HOW MANY TASKS WILL THERE BE?
Around 11-12 tasks are about right for a 2 to 3 hour race. Of course, it's going to depend on the time it takes to do each challenge. As with any new program like this, you should do a run-through with a few staff or volunteers to work out any potential problems.

ARE THERE ENOUGH SUPPLIES?

The thing here is that you don't want teams to get to a task and then have to wait. They need the opportunity to pass other teams. It's a race, after all. Therefore, you need to have enough supplies for all the teams to participate at once. At the very least, you should have enough supplies for half the number of teams.

WHO WILL BE SUPERVISING EACH TASK TO MAKE SURE THE TEAMS COMPLETE IT?

There are a few ways you can do this.

Activity Staff
Staff who don't have a team to supervise can run the challenges. Of course, you'll need enough staff for this. This option would be my first choice.

CITs
For summer camps that have a thriving CIT program, you can certainly use your CITs to supervise the challenges. If this is for a non-camp program, see if you can get some high school or college volunteers to help.

Camp Counselors
If the counselors who are already supervising each team are brought up to speed with all the challenges, they can ensure the tasks are being completed. The issue with this is that there is nobody keeping the counselors from assisting their teams or letting them skate by without completing the whole task. Even counselors can succumb to the peer pressure of kids.

HOW MANY PLAYERS WILL BE ON EACH TEAM?
In the Amazing Race it's teams of two. This is not ideal in a typical summer camp situation for a few reasons.
1. You would need a lot of staff if you wanted to effectively supervise the campers. However, if the campers are a bit older, this may be fine.
2. You would need a lot more supplies. More teams equal more challenge materials.
3. Since most camps have a mix of ages, teams of two would pose a problem. You don't want a team of 12 year-olds against a team of 7 year-olds. Pairing up different age groups could get messy as well.

Instead, you'll most likely want to put together teams of six or more. And if your camp has a mix of ages, your teams should represent that. While it may be awkward for a 12 and 7 year-old to be a two-person team, it would be fine to have two 12, two 9 and two 7 year-olds on one team. **The bigger the team, the easier it is for kids to accept the age differences of their teammates.**

To divide up teams you could have them pick numbers from a "hat" (each age group would pick from a different hat) or give counselors a sheet to assign their campers to the different teams. Then read the names out on race day.

Once you've answered the questions above, you'll need to create the route markers, the clue cards and envelopes, and the clue boxes you'll be using.

Route Markers

I have created a variety of bonus files for you. At the end of the book I tell you where to download them. In the files I have included a PDF with two Route Markers that you can print off. They are in the folder that accompanied this ebook. Print them out on sticker paper and stick them around camp or print them on regular paper and tape them up around camp.

Clue Cards

I have also included Clue Card templates in the same folder.

Envelopes

I have always used (and re-used) the 6"x9" brown clasp envelopes. But if you really want to go the extra mile, I suggest you check into Tear-ific envelopes. They can be found on Amazon.

Clue Boxes

Clue boxes aren't essential for the race, but they are neat to have all around camp. Imagine a team finishes a challenge and the staff person gives them their next envelope. The Route Info card tells them to go to the pool. They get to the pool and there is a black mailbox with a Route Marker on it. They reach in and pull out an envelope.

Don't want to spend the money on black mailboxes? I understand. You could use containers of any kind, as long as you tape a Route Marker to it.

The photo above is from ChicaAndJo.com. They have some neat ideas for putting on an Amazing Race. Check them out.

Okay, now it's time to assign staff to the various challenges and groups. After that, set-up the challenges and do a walk through to make sure everything is ready to go.

Everything good? Okay, time to decorate with country flags, themed décor or anything else you have.

PLANNING CHECKLIST

How long will the Race event last?
_____ 2-3 hours long
_____ All Day
_____ All Week (couple of hours each day)

Where will the Race take place?
_____ Our Own Premises
_____ Off Site

Will the Race be themed?
_____ Yes
_____ No
If yes, the theme will be _____

How many challenges will there be? _____

Who will supervise the challenges?
_____ Camp Staff
_____ CITs
_____ Self-supervised by staff with the teams
_____ Volunteers
_____ Teams will video themselves

What will be the size of the teams?
_____ 2-4 people
_____ 5-7 people
_____ 8-10 people
_____ 11+ people

Will the ages of the players be mixed on each team?
_____ Yes
_____ No

Who will supervise each team?
_____ Staff
_____ CITs
_____ Volunteers
_____ Nobody

General Race Supplies
_____ Route Markers
_____ Route Info Cards
_____ Challenge Cards
_____ Detour Cards
_____ Road Block Cards
_____ Intersection Cards
_____ Switch Passes
_____ Tokens
_____ Gnomes
_____ Express Passes
_____ Clue Boxes
_____ Decoration

Will you have an end of race Pit Stop style mat, or maybe a race ribbon to run through?
_____ Yes
_____ No

Challenge Name _____

Challenge Type

_____ Normal

_____ Detour

_____ Roadblock

_____ Intersection

_____ Other _____

How many of the players from each team need to complete the challenge?

_____ 1   _____ 2   _____ ALL

Description of Challenge

_____
_____
_____
_____
_____

Supplies Needed

(enough for at least half of the teams to do the challenge at the same time)

_____ _____ _____
_____ _____ _____
_____ _____ _____
_____ _____ _____

Person Supervising _____

IN-CAMP EXAMPLE (2-3 HOURS)

In this example, teams will be made up of 10 youth participants of mixed ages supervised by an adult. I am also using the "suggested addition" of Tokens and Transportation Hubs. You can find more ideas in the Suggested Additions chapter starting on page 96.

The players have been divided into their teams and assigned an adult (i.e. camp counselor, youth leader, volunteer, etc.). Allow them to choose a team name. You could also assign them a color and give each of them strips of cloth in that color to tie around their head or arm.

DISCUSSION OF RULES

Before the race, have the adults gather with the team they are supervising to give them the rules…

"There are a few guidelines that you'll need to know about so you don't get penalized during the race.

1. You must follow the instructions of each clue card exactly. For example, some challenges require only one or two people and others require the whole team.
2. The adult with you may not help your team in any way. So, do not ask for their advice or assistance. In fact, they will be the ones to make sure your team is doing everything correctly. Think of them as the camera person in the Amazing Race television show that follows the team.
3. Most of the challenges have enough supplies for all the teams to do them at the same time. However, there are a couple that only have supplies for about half of the teams. If there are no supplies for your team to do the challenge when you get there, you must wait patiently. First come, first serve.
4. There will be a reward for EVERY team that completes all 12 challenges. We want you to have fun. So, don't stress about what place you're in. Show everyone that you don't give up no matter what and complete the race.
5. Each challenge area will be marked by a Route Marker that looks like this (show Route Marker).
6. When you complete the challenge successfully, you will receive your next envelope.
7. Your first envelope is waiting for you in the dining hall. It is under the sign of your team name (or color). No envelope may be opened until the whole team is present."

PRE-RACE ANNOUNCEMENT

The following was written using the original speech by Phil on the first The Amazing Race as a template. Change it to suit your camp and race. This can be done live by someone on the leadership staff or it can be a pre-recorded video.

"We are gathered here at Camp Wally, a camp steeped in tradition and the host to 15 teams full of campers who have decided to take a break from their everyday lives and embark on a one week journey of summer camp AND a race around that camp for prizes and glory.

Contestants will be racing without the benefit of adult assistance, computers or cellphones. Their greatest resource will be each other as they circle the camp in teams of ten.

[announce each team by their team name]

Can your team withstand the stress of working together for 3 whole hours?

Who will muster the right combination of brains, brawn and teamwork to win bragging rights and get their team photo posted on the Wall of Champions?

These are the questions weighing most heavily as we get ready to begin...The Amazing Race!

[Play theme music that you downloaded from iTunes or Amazon. It's worth the dollar or two.]

Well, in just a few minutes you'll begin a race that will circle the camp. Along the way, you'll be required to complete a number of tasks. Now some of these will be physically challenging, others will challenge your mind. Once you start, you need to complete your tasks as fast as you can, because the first team to get to the Pit Stop will win.

Does everybody understand that?

When I give you the word, you'll race to the dining hall and find the table with your team color. Once your whole team is seated, you may open your first envelope.

I want to wish all of you the best of luck.

GO!

THE RACE

The first card says:

Your team has 10 tokens for this race. Use them wisely. Your first challenge is to complete the puzzle in front of you. When you are finished, raise your hand and you will receive your next clue.

After the team completes the puzzle the supervising staff person checks it and gives them their next clue card. Inside is a Route Info card.

Route Info Card:

WooHoo! You did it!

Now your team needs to catch a flight, or taxi, or just stay on foot.

Go to the transportation hub and choose your transportation. Where's the transportation hub? Where would you find modes of transportation here at camp?

When the team gets to the transportation hub (in this case, the parking lot) they must find the clue box for their next clue card.

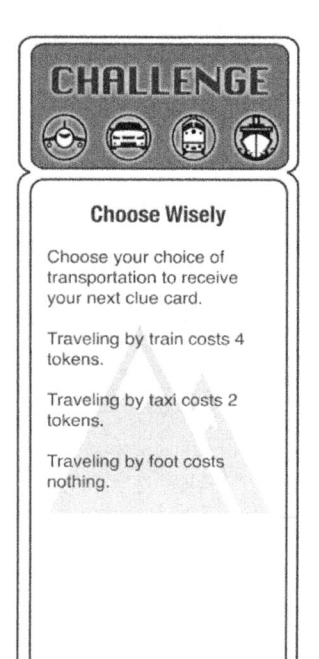

Challenge Card:
Choose wisely.

Choose your choice of transportation to receive your next clue card.

Traveling by train costs 4 tokens.

Traveling by taxi costs 2 tokens.

Traveling by foot costs nothing.

Once they have chosen (purchased) their transportation they will receive their next Route Info Card.

Just to be clear, teams won't actually travel by train or taxi. They will receive clues based on their transportation choice. The more tokens they spend, the easier the clue. They may also incur a waiting period based on their transportation choice.

By Train
If they choose to travel by "train" there is **no wait** and their Route Info Card will **tell them exactly where to go**.

By Taxi
If they choose to travel by "taxi", they must **wait one minute** before receiving their Route Info Card and solve a **fairly easy clue** to determine where to go.

By Foot
If they choose to travel by foot, they must **wait two minutes** for their Route Info Card and solve a **more difficult clue** to determine their next location.

Here is an example of what may be on the Route Info Card.

Train Card:	*Go to Pool*

Taxi Card:	*When the weather is hot,*
We all want to get cool.
Grab some special clothing,
And jump into a _____.

By Foot Card:	*Red shirts with white crosses,*
Worn by those in a specific vocation.
Tiles, board, a hole with water,
Things you'll see at your next location

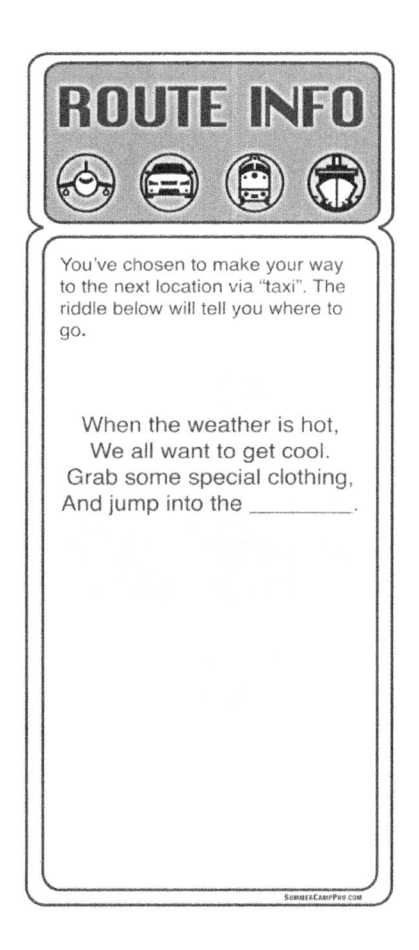

ROUTE INFO

You've chosen to make your way to the next location via "taxi". The riddle below will tell you where to go.

When the weather is hot,
We all want to get cool.
Grab some special clothing,
And jump into the _____.

Once at the pool, teams must find the clue box to receive their next card telling them about their challenge.

After they complete the challenge, teams will receive their next Route Info card. This goes on for the rest of the game. Here is a quick example overview of the race cards.

1. Challenge Card #1
2. Route Info Card
3. Challenge Card #2
4. Route Info Card
5. Challenge Card #3
6. Route Info Card
7. Detour Card
8. Route Info Card
9. Challenge Card #4
10. Route Info Card
11. Intersection Card
12. Route Info Card
13. Challenge Card #5
14. Route Info Card
15. Challenge Card #6
16. Route Info Card
17. Challenge Card #7
18. Route Info Card
19. Detour Card
20. Route Info Card
21. Challenge Card #8
22. Route Info Card
23. Challenge Card #9
24. Route Info Card

WEEK-LONG RACE

If you want the Race to go throughout the week you may want to "visit" a different country each day. You could have anywhere between 4-12 challenges daily. For example, teams would visit China on Monday and complete challenges that you might see in China. Take a look at the Around the World variation on page 79.

IN-CAMP CHALLENGES

There are plenty of challenges you can create. It depends on your facilities, program equipment, staffing and number of participants. When creating your challenges keep the following thoughts in mind.

The challenges should take some time and be, well, challenging.
If you set up challenges that are quick and easy, the race will not be nearly as fun and the team that gets the early lead will keep it. You want teams to have a chance to pass each other and the best way to make that happen is through challenges that take time and/or are a bit difficult.

Put some distance in between the challenges.
You don't want teams to know exactly where they place in the race and how far ahead, or behind, other teams are. The best way to do this is to have the challenges spread throughout your property. If teams are running back and forth and all around, it becomes difficult to know who is in first and how far ahead they are. As opposed to having all the challenges in a row, one after another.

Add some Detours and Roadblocks.
Going from one challenge to the next can be a lot of fun for players, but when you add in unexpected twists, that takes the game to another level.

On the following pages, I have given you some ideas for challenges. I have written out the supplies needed and what to write on the clue cards.

The challenges are divided into General Challenges, Roadblocks, Detours and Intersections.

PLEASE NOTE: Time penalties are often given if the players are unable to complete their challenge. This is better than having teams attempt a challenge, that they cannot seem to complete, over and over again. That would just be frustrating for the players and any team that may be waiting for their turn to use the equipment.

I have added specific time penalty lengths for those challenges, but you can, of course, change any of them to a time that best suits your event.

GENERAL CHALLENGES

THE AMAZING RACE
GENERAL TASKS

The Amazing Race is made up of mostly general tasks/challenges. Later in the book there are example of roadblocks and detours. Here are some ideas for challenges that you can do at camp.

CHALLENGE

Some Assembly Required

Choose a tent box. Take out the equipment and set the tent up properly. Once the set-up has been approved by the supervising staff person, take it down and put it back in the box it came in.

When the box has been closed, your team will receive the next clue.

TOASTED MALLOWS

Description:
> This challenge has teams build a fire and roast marshmallows. After that, they must put the fire out before moving on.

Supplies Needed:
- Multiple fire pits
- Firewood
- Matches
- Marshmallows
- Sticks or rods (to cook marshmallows on)
- Water
- Laminated instruction cards on building a fire and putting it out

Instructions to be written on the card:

> TOASTED MALLOWS
>
> Roast one marshmallow for each team member. Build a fire, roast the marshmallows, eat them, and put out the fire correctly. You will find laminated instruction cards on building a fire and putting it out at the fire pit.
>
> If everything is done correctly, your team will receive the next clue.

IT'S PUZZLING

Description:

This challenge is pretty straightforward; choose a puzzle and put it together. After the puzzle is complete, teams must put the puzzle pieces back in the box. They will want to unhook each piece so that if any other team chooses that puzzle, they won't have an advantage with pieces of the puzzle already together.

Supplies Needed:
- Multiple puzzles (with 30-50 pieces – all puzzles should have the same number of pieces)

Instructions to be written on the card:

IT'S PUZZLING

Complete one of the puzzles to get your next clue. All puzzles have the same number of pieces. When finished, have it checked by the supervising staff person.

Once checked, take apart the puzzle and return the pieces to the box. Take the box to the supervising staff person to get your next clue.

LEADING THE BLIND

Description:
>This one takes some good communication, especially if there are multiple teams going at once.
>
>One person is blindfolded, and the rest of the team must stay behind a designated rope and verbally give directions to the blindfolded player.
>
>The task is for the blindfolded player to grab one of the garden gnomes and return it to the team.
>
>To add a little excitement, two of the gnomes have a special mark on the bottom. If the team gets one of those "prize gnomes" they will receive a small gift (candy, buttons, first into the dining hall at lunch, etc.). I prefer prizes that are separate from the game, meaning that it does not affect the game play (i.e. bonus time or special hints).

Supplies Needed:
- Multiple blindfolds
- Rope or cones (to create a boundary line for teams)
- Gnome statues (or other object, like team flags or stuffed animals)
- Prizes for two teams (the special prizes can be candy, stickers, small toys, etc.)

Instructions to be written on the card:

LEADING THE BLIND

Blindfold one team member. The rest of the team must stay behind the designated line. Verbally lead the blindfold player to any of the gnome figures, and then guide them back to the team. They cannot take their blindfold off until they have returned.

Two of the gnomes have a special prize written on the bottom. Choose carefully, as you can only retrieve one gnome.

Turn in the gnome to the supervising staff person to get your next clue.

ALL FOR ONE

Description:
>You may or may not want to include fitness-type challenges, but if you do, this is a simple one. It includes a series of physical exercises. All players can participate, but only one at a time. If a team has a couple of super fit athletes, they can take a brunt of the challenge. If the whole team is equally fit, then they can all share the workload.

Supplies Needed:
- None

Instructions to be written on the card:

>ALL FOR ONE
>
>As a team, you must complete 200 sit-ups, 100 push-ups and 25 burpees. Only one player may go at a time.
>
>Once completed, your team will receive the next clue.

WHERE THERE'S A WILL

Description:
>Teams are given a compass and some instructions. You can make the instructions as easy or difficult as you want. You may want to include a card on how to read a compass, as most players will not know how.
>
>The directions should lead the team to a clue box. Alternatively, you could paint rocks with different numbers. Then place those rocks around the area. The directions, if followed properly, will lead the team to a specific rock with a specific number. The team then tells the supervising staff person the correct number to get their next clue.
>
>The reason for the multiple rocks with different numbers is to keep teams from just running around and looking for the rock that has a number on it (or the clue box).

Supplies Needed:
- Multiple compasses
- Cards with instructions
    - Example: Go west 100 steps, then southwest another 50 steps

Instructions to be written on the card:

WHERE THERE'S A WILL

Follow the directions on the card with a compass to make your way to the next clue.

SHOW ME SOME ID

Description:
>If you'd like to add some outdoor education to the race, this is a challenge you'll like.
>
>Teams will have to identify which tree is which by using the supplied sheet of paper. If you don't have 3-5 different types of trees on your property you could include shrubs, or you could set up animal tracks and do the same thing.

Supplies Needed:
- Quiz sheets (paper with the names identifying traits of five different trees. Teams must put the letter of the tree next to its name on the sheet.)
- Multiple clipboards
- Pens or pencils
- Laminated sheets or wood blocks with letters a-e (place one of the letters in front of each of the five trees.)

Instructions to be written on the card:

>SHOW ME SOME ID
>
>Properly identify each of the five different trees by using the identifying traits on the quiz sheet. Write down the correct letter next to the tree name on the provided sheet.
>
>Check with the supervising staff person to see if you're correct. They will let you know how many you have correct but not which ones they are.
>
>Once you have correctly identified all five trees, your team will receive the next clue.

SOME ASSEMBLY REQUIRED

Description:
> The idea of setting up a tent seems easy. For anyone that has actually set up a tent, you know that it can be deceivingly difficult. Of course, some are easier than others.
>
> Teams must properly set up a tent and then put it away.

Supplies Needed:
- Multiple tents

Instructions to be written on the card:

> SOME ASSEMBLY REQUIRED
>
> Choose a tent box (or bag). Take out the equipment and set the tent up properly.
>
> Once the set-up has been approved by the supervising staff person, take it down and put it back in the box (or bag) it came in. When the box has been closed (or the bag has been zipped up), your team will receive the next clue.

SCAVENGING FOR NATURE

Description:
>Kids love scavenger hunts. Teams must find 15 items to get their next clue. I am partial to items that are a bit abstract like "something rough" and "something cool", but a list of specific items (i.e. a red leaf, a rock, a pinecone, etc.) is good, too.

Supplies Needed:
- Lists of nature items (for example: acorn, pinecone, something blue, something smooth, etc.)
- Paper bags

Instructions to be written on the card:

> SCAVENGING FOR NATURE
>
> Get a list of items from the supervising staff person. Gather all 15 items on the list.
>
> Once collected, take the items to the supervising staff person to get your next clue.

CAN YOU HACK IT?

Description:
This is a team challenge where everyone must kick a footbag at least once.

This can be a very difficult challenge. The larger the team, the more challenging it will be. You may decide that only half the team must kick the bag before it touches the ground, or you may allow the bag to touch the ground once without having to start over. Ages of the kids will play a big role as well.

Supplies Needed:
- Multiple Hacky Sacks

Instructions to be written on the card:

CAN YOU HACK IT?

As a team, juggle the hacky sack. Each team member must kick it at least once without it hitting the ground or using hands. Begin by kicking it.

Once the task has been accomplished, your team will receive the next clue.

BEANS IN A JAR

Description:
> Fill a jar with jellybeans and let teams guess how many there are. If they get within 20 of the actual number, they get their next clue. If not, they must wait one minute before guessing again.
>
> To keep the number secret, have team write their guesses on a piece of paper rather than saying it out loud.

Supplies Needed:
- Jar
- Jellybeans (enough to fill the jar)
- Pens or pencils
- Paper

Instructions to be written on the card:

> BEANS IN A JAR
>
> Write down a guess on how many jellybeans are in the jar and give it to the supervising staff member.
>
> If your guess is within 20 jellybeans, your team will receive the next clue. If your guess is not within 20 jellybeans, you must wait 60 seconds before submitting your next guess.

FROZEN

Description:

> Teams must free an object from a block of ice. They cannot throw or drop the block. They will need to use the heat from their hands, and they can use rocks to chip away at it.
>
> It doesn't matter what object you freeze in the ice as long as it doesn't float (you want the object to freeze in the middle of the ice block). Using milk jugs is good for creating blocks of ice. Freeze the first half. Add your item. Then add more water. Now cut away the container. If you use plastic containers, there is a chance they will crack, and the unfrozen water will spill out all over. Check online for instructions that best suit you.

Supplies Needed:
- Small item frozen in a block of ice (one ice block per team)

Instructions to be written on the card:

> FROZEN
>
> Choose a block of ice. Free the item from the block of ice. You may not throw or drop the block of ice. You may not use water to melt the ice.
>
> Once you have freed the item, take it to the supervising staff member for your next clue.

IT'S FREE TO THROW

Description:
>Each team must make 10 free throws. While not every player must make a free throw, no player can make more than 3 baskets. This is to make sure that a really good basketball shooter doesn't give a team an unfair advantage.
>
>On the flip side, lots of kids are not athletes. That's why I don't like making it so that each player has to sink a free throw. Everybody has their strengths and weaknesses. There's no need to embarrass anyone.

Supplies Needed:
- Multiple basketballs
- Multiple basketball hoops

Instructions to be written on the card:

>IT'S FREE TO THROW
>
>As a team, make 10 free throws. No player can make more than 3 free throws.
>
>When your team has finished, you will receive the next clue.

ABRACADABRA

Description:
> Each team will choose one player to learn and perform a magic trick. There are lots of prop tricks that are really easy to perform. All they need to do is read the instructions.
>
> Having multiple props available makes this challenge more interesting. You could also have decks of cards with written instructions for different tricks.

Supplies Needed:
- Multiple magic tricks (beginner's tricks that come with instructions)

Instructions to be written on the card:

> ABRACADABRA
>
> Choose one of the magic tricks before you. Each trick comes with instructions. After practicing, have one team member perform the illusion for the supervising staff member. If they are satisfied that you have mastered the trick, your team will receive the next clue.

HUNT EGGSTRAVAGANZA

Description:
> This is an egg hunt. You will need to have four different colors of eggs and a few golden eggs. They should be hidden pretty well, not just tossed around and visible. The idea is to have the teams actually search for eggs.
>
> Teams must find one egg of each of the four colors to move on. Alternatively, they can turn in a golden egg if they find it. If they find a golden egg, not only do they not have to find the other colors, they also get a prize. Prizes can be anything from treats to an advantage in the game.

Supplies Needed:
- Plastic Easter eggs (varying colors)
- One golden Easter egg

Instructions to be written on the card:

> HUNT EGGSTRAVAGANZA
>
> Search the surrounding area for four Easter eggs, one of each color (blue, red, green and yellow), or one golden egg. If you find a golden egg you do not have to find the other colors.
>
> Give the eggs to the supervising staff member to receive your next clue.

ALL WRAPPED UP

Description:

> Provide wrapping paper, bows, ribbon, tape and a bunch of boxes. Each player must do a decent job in wrapping a box after watching a demonstration. The demonstration can be on video or given live by a staff member.

Supplies Needed:
- Wrapping paper
- Ribbon
- Bows
- Scotch tape

Instructions to be written on the card:

> ALL WRAPPED UP
>
> After watching a demonstration, each member of your team must properly wrap a box using wrapping paper, ribbon, a bow and tape.
>
> Once each of the boxes are wrapped correctly, your team will receive its next clue.

PUTT IT THERE, MY FIREND

Description:
> If you have disc golf baskets available, this is a great task to add. Decide on a putting distance based on the age of the campers and mark it off with cones or rope. It's fine to have different distances based on the different ages. As teams come in, assign them to one particular area to toss from and give them one disc.
>
> Half of the players from each team must make the putt. If a player doesn't make it, they can try again until they do.

Supplies Needed:
- Disc golf basket
- Multiple discs
- Rope or cones (to show where to put from)

Instructions to be written on the card:

> PUTT IT THERE, MY FRIEND
>
> Half of the players on your team must throw a disc into the basket from the putting line.
>
> Once all putts have been made, your team will receive the next clue.

ALL TIED UP

Description:

    This task requires all players to learn four knots. Once they all feel as though they have it, the supervising adult will test each of them by asking them to tie a specific knot.

    Once each player has successfully tied the knot they were asked to tie, they will get their next clue. For each person that is unsuccessful, a 20 second penalty will be assessed before they can get their next clue. In other words, if three players didn't tie their knot correctly, the wait time would be 60 seconds.

Supplies Needed:
- Laminated cards with instructions on knot tying
- Multiple rope pieces to practice and test on

Instructions to be written on the card:

    ALL TIED UP

    Each team member must learn how to tie four different knots. Once each player is confident that they know how to tie all four knots, you may take the test.

    The supervising staff person will ask each of the players to tie a specific knot. If everyone does their knot correctly, you'll receive the next clue. A penalty will be given for each person that is unsuccessful.

CHARADES

Description:
>Each player chooses a word from a bag and acts it out without talking. When the team guesses the word, the next player goes until everyone has had a turn.

Supplies Needed:
- Slips of paper with names of movies, tv shows, food, places, people, etc.
- Paper bag

Instructions to be written on the card:

>CHARADES
>
>Each team member must choose a slip of paper out of the bag and get their team to say the word on the paper using charades. Clues must be given without talking or making sounds of any kind.
>
>Once each player has gotten their team to say the correct word, you'll receive your next clue.

SHIP BUILDERS

Description:
> Teams are tasked to turn a cardboard box into a boat and row it across a pool. This is a popular activity at camps, colleges and elsewhere. Hint: the more duct tape teams use, the better.

Supplies Needed:
- Large cardboard boxes
- Lots of duct tape
- Paddles

Instructions to be written on the card:

> DON'T ROCK THE BOAT
>
> Use one cardboard box and make it sturdy enough to carry a team member across the pool. If the player reaches the other side of the pool without sinking, the team will receive its next clue. If the boat sinks, however, the team must take a 10-minute penalty.

TALK TO THE HAND

Description:
It's best if you have a staff member that knows sign language for this one.

Each player must learn to sign their name as well as signing "I love the Amazing Race".

Supplies Needed:
- Instruction cards of alphabet in American Sign Language (ASL)
- Instruction cards of words in ASL needed for the sentence

Instructions to be written on the card:

> TALK TO THE HAND
>
> Using the provided materials, each player must learn the letters of their name in sign language, as well as how to sign, "I love the Amazing Race."
>
> Once each player can prove to the supervising staff member that they can sign their name and the sentence, the team will receive the next clue.

DO YOU REMEMBER?

Description:
>A popular task during the last leg of The Amazing Race show is to put the countries that the teams visited in order. If, in your race, you had the teams "visit" different countries, you could do the same. If not, simply write each challenge on a card and have them place those cards in order.

Supplies Needed:
- Multiple sets of laminated cards representing all the challenges (or countries)

Instructions to be written on the card:

>DO YOU REMEMBER?
>
>Put in order the challenges you faced in this Race.
>
>Once the challenges are in the proper order, your team will receive the final clue.

ROADBLOCKS

Road Blocks are tasks that only one team member (or two in some cases when the teams are larger) may perform. Once the player is chosen, teams may not switch, unless they use a "Switch Pass". You can read more about Switch Passes on page 99.

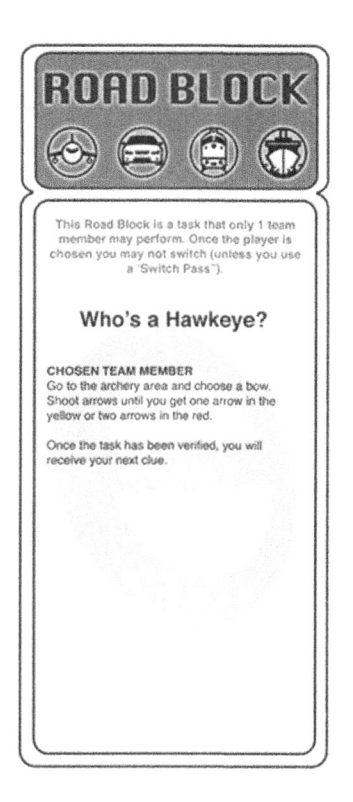

On the Road Block cards, you may want to have the details of the actual challenge on the back or on a separate card. That way, the teams will choose their player(s) before they know what the challenge is. This is staying more in line with the show. So, in this example, the front of the card would say WHO'S A HAWKEYE? The team would choose their player given that one clue. Then they would turn the card over to read about the task.

You may also want to add the stipulation that no player may do more than one Road Block.

A BIRD'S PARADISE

Description:
> The chosen player must put together a bird house from a kit. No need to paint it.

Supplies Needed:
- Multiple pre-cut birdhouses with instructions (check oriental trading for inexpensive, easy-to-assemble birdhouses)
- Multiple tool sets

Instructions to be written on the card:

> WHO'S HANDY AND LIKES BIRDS?
>
> CHOSEN TEAM MEMBER
> Assemble a pre-cut birdhouse. All the tools and instructions are provided
>
> Once the birdhouse is assembled correctly, you will receive the next clue.

YOUR NUMBER'S UP

Description:
    The designated player works out a math problem. That number is how many jumping jacks the rest of the team must perform. The jumping jacks can be performed by one person or multiple people, but only one may jump at a time.

Supplies Needed:
- Posted math problem (This could be on butcher paper or a dry erase board.)
- Separated space for math work
- Paper
- Pens or pencils

Instructions to be written on the card:

WHO LOVES NUMBERS?

CHOSEN TEAM MEMBER
Go to the designated area, while the rest of your team waits here. Work out the math equation that is on the board.

The answer to the equation is the number of jumping jacks the rest of the team must perform. Your team can have one person do all of them or divide the jumping jacks between players, but only one team member may jump at a time.

Once the jumping jacks have been completed the supervising staff person will tell you if the math answer is correct. If it is, your team will receive the next clue. If it is not, the chosen mathematician must try again. At that time, your team may choose a different person to work out the equation.

1982

Description:
> This one is simple. Find the penny that is dated 1982 (or whatever year you choose) out of a jar of pennies. There should only be a few of that year in the jar.

Supplies Needed:
- Multiple jars or buckets
- Lots of pennies
- One to three 1982 pennies per jar

Instructions to be written on the card:

> WHICH TWO PLAYERS LOVE THE 80s?
>
> CHOSEN TEAM MEMBERS
> Choose one of the jars of pennies. Search for a penny dated 1982. Place all the other pennies back in the jar.
>
> Give the 1982 penny to the supervising staff person to receive your next clue.

HEADS UP

Description:
> One player hits a ball off a tee, and another must catch it behind a designated line. The ball cannot touch the ground. Players will continue until a ball is caught.

Supplies Needed:
- Multiple tees
- Multiple bats
- Multiple balls (using tennis balls or whiffle balls negate the need for baseball gloves.)
- Rope or cones (to create a boundary line for catchers)

Instructions to be written on the card:

> WHICH TWO PLAYERS LIKE TEE?
>
> CHOSEN TEAM MEMBERS
> Choose one person to hit and one to catch.
>
> The batter will hit a ball off a tee. The catcher must stand behind the designated line. The ball cannot hit the ground before being caught. Any ball that is caught in front of the designated line does not count.
>
> Once a ball is caught behind the line without hitting the ground first, your team will be given their next clue.

FLAGS AHOY

Description:
> Two players must kayak out to a buoy and retrieve their flag. Each team is given one kayak and one paddle.

Supplies Needed:
- One flag for each team (may be color coded if teams have a specific team color)
- Multiple canoes or kayaks
- Multiple paddles
- Route marker (to attach to designated buoy)

Instructions to be written on the card:

> WHICH TWO PLAYERS GET THE PADDLE?
>
> CHOSEN TEAM MEMBERS
> Choose a kayak and one paddle. Yes, one paddle for your team of two, not for each player.
>
> Paddle to the designated buoy, retrieve your flag, and return to shore to get your next clue.

IT'S A TOSS UP

Description:
> This is a basic balloon toss. People of all ages love a good balloon toss. The two designated players must toss the water balloon back and forth 4 times. Make sure you have plenty of water balloons ready.
>
> I would suggest that after three failed attempts, the team is given a three-minute penalty instead of continuously using up water balloons.

Supplies Needed:
- Multiple water balloons
- Ropes or cones (to create lines for players to stand behind)

Instructions to be written on the card:

> WHICH TWO PLAYERS CAN TOSS?
>
> CHOSEN TEAM MEMBERS
> Toss a water balloon back and forth 4 times from the designated distances without bursting the balloon.
>
> If successful, you will receive your next clue. If not, try again.

HAWKEYE

Description:
> The designated player must use an archery bow to get one arrow in the yellow or two in the red to move on.

Supplies Needed:
- Archery gear and range
- One or two balloons per target

Instructions to be written on the card:

> WHO'S A HAWKEYE?
>
> CHOSEN TEAM MEMBER
> Go to the archery area and choose a bow. Shoot arrows until you get one arrow in the yellow or two arrows in the red.
>
> Once the task has been verified, you will receive your next clue.

CARD NINJA

Description:
> While difficult, this is not an impossible task at all. The designated player is given a deck of cards and must throw (with a flick of the wrist) and stick one of them into a watermelon from a few feet away.
>
> Once a card has stuck in the watermelon, the team can move on. However, if the player has gone through all 52 cards, a two-minute time penalty is assigned to the team. You may want to allow teams to switch players after every 10th or 15th card.

Supplies Needed:
- Multiple watermelon halves
- Multiple decks of playing cards
- Rope or cones (to create a throwing line)

Instructions to be written on the card:

> WHO'S A NINJA?
>
> CHOSEN TEAM MEMBER
> Stand behind the throwing line and throw playing cards one at a time at the watermelon halves.
>
> Once you stick a card into a watermelon, you will receive your next clue.

ZIP IT

Description:
> The designated player must land a Koosh ball or bean bag in a specific area (hula hoop or tarp is best). Because of the forward momentum, the thrown object often lands in the right spot but then rolls off. Players will most likely need a few chances to get it in. If after five turns they still have not landed it, give the team a time penalty.

Supplies Needed:
- Zip line
- Multiple harnesses
- Multiple Koosh balls
- Hula hoops or tarp (lay out a few hula hoops or one tarp)

Instructions to be written on the card:

> WHO LIKES HEIGHTS?
>
> CHOSEN TEAM MEMBER
> Get harnessed up and go down the zipline. You must land a Koosh ball inside of one of the hula hoops (or onto the tarp).
>
> If unsuccessful, you must try again. You get five attempts before receiving a time penalty. When you've accomplished the task, you will receive your next clue.

RING-A-DING

Description:
> The designated player must retrieve three pool rings from the bottom. This is an easy task for most players. More time will probably be taken getting in and out of their bathing suit.
>
> Don't forget to remind them that there is no running around the pool.

Supplies Needed:
- Pool
- Multiple pool rings
- Cowbell

Instructions to be written on the card:

> WHO CAN HOLD THEIR BREATH?
>
> CHOSEN TEAM MEMBER
> Change into your bathing suit and retrieve three rings from the bottom of the pool, one at a time.
>
> When all three rings have been retrieved, ring the cowbell to receive your next clue.

GOO GOO

Description:
>Food challenges are fun to watch. While you could have players eat insects or cow tongue, baby food can be just as intimidating.
>
>The designated player chooses a jar of baby food and eats it. It's that simple. I like to take the labels off so the players can't see what flavor it is.

Supplies Needed:
- A variety of jarred baby food

Instructions to be written on the card:

>WHO ENJOYS ACTING LIKE A BABY?
>
>CHOSEN TEAM MEMBER
>Put on a bib, choose one of the jars of baby food, and eat all the food in it.
>
>Once finished, you will receive your next clue.

A BUG'S LIFE

Description:
>Insects make for a great eating challenge. There are plenty of edible options online, and possibly at local ethnic grocers.
>
>The designated player simply needs to eat the insect in whatever form it takes (cookie, seasoned, chocolate covered, raw, BBQed, etc.)

Supplies Needed:
- Edible Insects (This can be anything from meal worm cookies to seasoned crickets.)

Instructions to be written on the card:

>WHO'S HUNGER IS BUGGIN' THEM?
>
>CHOSEN TEAM MEMBER
>Eat this insect delicacy to receive your next clue.

MARSHMALLOW ATTACK

Description:
    Marshmallow shooters are a lot of fun and easily assembled (once they are created out of PVC pipe). Shooting them, on the other hand, takes a little practice. A demonstration by an adult may be needed.

    The designated player shoots mini marshmallows at a target. I like to use action figures or green army men. Once the target has been hit (or knocked over) the team can move on.

Supplies Needed:
- Multiple homemade marshmallow shooters (made from PVC pipe)
- Mini-marshmallows
- Targets (plastic army men work great)
- An assembled shooter as the example

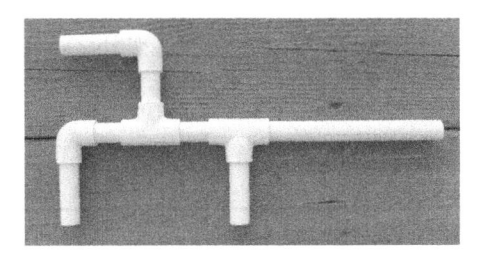

Instructions to be written on the card:

> WHO CAN STAY ON TARGET?
>
> CHOSEN TEAM MEMBER
> Assemble the PVC pipe marshmallow shooter and hit the designated target by shooting a mini-marshmallow at it.
>
> Once the target has been hit by the properly assembled shooter, you will receive your next clue.

YOU SPIN ME RIGHT ROUND

Description:
> For some kids this will be a snap. For others, this may be the most frustrating challenge ever. The player must keep a hula hoop spinning around their waste for a full minute.

Supplies Needed:
- Multiple Hula Hoops
- Stopwatch

Instructions to be written on the card:

> YOU SPIN ME RIGHT ROUND
>
> CHOSEN TEAM MEMBER
> Keep a hula hoop up and spinning around your waist for 60 seconds without stopping.
>
> Once complete, you will receive the next clue.

DETOURS

**THE AMAZING RACE
DETOURS**

A detour is the choice between two tasks. Teams will read each task and then choose the one they think their team can do the quickest. They can switch tasks if they decide the one they picked proves too difficult.

Place the tasks at different areas of the camp. This keeps teams from seeing the challenges before choosing one. It also keeps them from knowing how well the teams who chose the other task are doing. It all adds to the excitement of the race.

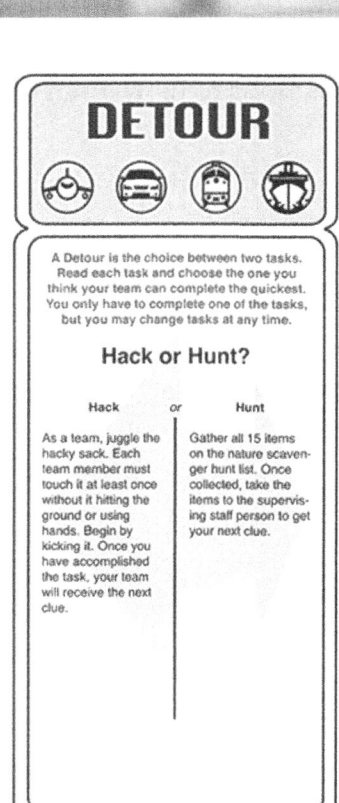

DETOUR

A Detour is the choice between two tasks. Read each task and choose the one you think your team can complete the quickest. You only have to complete one of the tasks, but you may change tasks at any time.

Hack or Hunt?

Hack *or* **Hunt**

As a team, juggle the hacky sack. Each team member must touch it at least once without it hitting the ground or using hands. Begin by kicking it. Once you have accomplished the task, your team will receive the next clue.

Gather all 15 items on the nature scavenger hunt list. Once collected, take the items to the supervising staff person to get your next clue.

BRAINS OR BRAWN?

Supplies Needed:
- Random items in a room
- Four different tests on paper that ask questions like, What color is the shoe?, Where is the teddy bear sitting?, and What year was the quarter minted?
- Pens
- Lots of sandbags or other heavy items (2 or 3 per player)

Instructions to be written on the card:

> BRAINS
>
> Go into the designated room and memorize the items that are spread out inside. Come back out and request the test. You will be given one of four different test sheets with five questions.
>
> You may not go back into the room for the answers. This is a memory test.
>
> Write down your answers and turn the sheet into the supervising staff member. If any answer is incorrect, go back into the room and memorize everything. Then come back out and take test #2. Get all five answers correct, you'll receive your next clue.
>
> BRAWN
>
> Carry 20 sandbags 100 yards. This is a team event, which means that it doesn't matter how many sandbags each player carries; you just need to get all the bags to the designated area.

PACK IT OR STACK IT?

Supplies Needed:
- Hundreds of nickels
- Large suitcases (all the same size – or make it a little harder with trunks)
- Multiple boxes (different sizes) – pack the suitcases with the boxes ahead of time so that you know which boxes to provide for each suitcase. It should be a tight fit.

Instructions to be written on the card:

PACK IT

Pack one suitcase with all the different shaped boxes provided. You must be able to zip the suitcase closed to receive your next clue.

STACK IT

Stack 50 nickels. They must remain stacked unassisted for five seconds to receive your next clue.

TIE IT OR FIND IT?

Supplies Needed:
- Laminated cards with instructions on knot tying
- Multiple rope pieces to practice and test on
- Multiple buckets
- Thousands of pennies

Instructions to be written on the card:

> TIE IT
>
> Learn how to tie the four knots on the provided cards. Once each player is confident that they know how to tie all four knots, you may take the test.
>
> The supervising staff person will ask each of the players to tie a specific knot. If everyone does their knot correctly, you'll receive the next clue.
>
> FIND IT
>
> Choose one of the buckets of pennies. Search for a penny dated 1982.
>
> Once you have found the penny, return all the pennies to the bucket. After that, you'll receive your next clue.

DOG OR CAT?

Supplies Needed:
- Cocoa Puffs for the dog food
- Dog bowls (or regular bowls)
- White cake with grey food coloring (this is for the cat food – crumble the cake and clump it up in a litter box – there are recipes online for this…crazy, huh?)
- Litter boxes (or plastic boxes)

Instructions to be written on the card:

> DOG
>
> Eat the food that is in the dog bowl. Once your team has eaten it all, you'll receive the next clue.
>
> CAT
>
> Eat the food that is in the litter box. Once your team has eaten it all, you'll receive the next clue.

HACK OR HUNT?

Supplies Needed:
- Multiple hacky sacks
- Lists of nature items (for example: acorn, pinecone, something blue, etc.)
- Paper bags

Instructions to be written on the card:

> HACK
>
> As a team, juggle the hacky sack. Each team member must touch it at least once without it hitting the ground or using hands. Begin by kicking it.
>
> Once the task has been accomplished, your team will receive the next clue.
>
> HUNT
>
> Get a list of items from the supervising staff person. Gather all 15 items on the list.
>
> Once collected, take the items to the supervising staff person to get your next clue.

INTERSECTIONS

**THE AMAZING RACE
INTERSECTIONS**

An Intersection is a task where two teams must work together to accomplish it.

Most teams will just work with the first team they can get together with. However, if the teams are playing a strategic game of alliances, they may wait until a specific team shows up before taking on the task. This may or may not be a good strategy.

I have provided four examples of Intersection tasks. Tasks might require all or many of the players, or it may just need a couple from each team to work together.

HUMAN ALPHABET

Description:
> Players must work together to create a word with their bodies. This can be done standing up or laying on the ground. This is a great photo opportunity.
>
> The word you choose should be the same for all the groups. Keep in mind that many letters will require two people or more. AMAZING RACE could take 18 players or more to spell out.

Supplies Needed:
- None (besides the players themselves)

Instructions to be written on the card:

> HUMAN ALPHABET
>
> Using just your bodies, spell out WINTER. You may remain standing or you can lie on the ground.
>
> Once the task has been verified, you will receive your next clue.

TELEPHONE FACE TIME

Description:
> Most of us have played telephone as a kid. In this version motions and gestures will replace words.
>
> All the players line-up, one behind the other. The last player in line turns around and the supervising adult gives them a series of motions and gestures. It could be motions that tell a story or just a bunch of random movements. The player then turns around, taps the next person in line to face them, and demonstrates the movements in order.
>
> When the first person in line has been given all the moves, they will perform it for the adult who will judge if it's good enough for them to move on. If it's not, both teams must wait out a two-minute penalty.

Supplies Needed:
- None

Instructions to be written on the card:

> TELEPHONE FACE TIME
>
> Line up one behind another. The task supervisor will give the last player in the line a series of movements to memorize. That player will then tap the shoulder of the person in front of them and perform the series of motions and gestures.
>
> The first person in line must perform it correctly for the task master for the teams to receive their next clue.

TEAM JIGSAW

Description:
>A bag of jigsaw puzzle pieces from two different puzzles are given to the group. Each team must put together their own puzzle. They can help each other, but neither team can move on until both puzzles are completed.
>
>The more puzzle pieces there are, the more difficult the challenge. Smaller puzzles of 30-50 pieces are good.

Supplies Needed:
- Tables or hard floor spaces to build the puzzles on
- One puzzle per team
- Bags to put the puzzle pieces of two puzzles in

Instructions to be written on the card:

>TEAM JIGSAW
>
>In the bag you will find puzzle pieces of two puzzles. Each team must work together to complete their own puzzle, but members from the other team may help once their own puzzle is complete.
>
>When both puzzles are put together completely, your teams will receive the next clue.

WATER BALLOON TOSS

Description:
> In this task each team chooses three players. They can switch out players at any time.
>
> Three different distances are set up using tape, rope or cones. One person from team A tosses a water balloon to the player from team B from the shortest distance. The player from team B then tosses it back. If the balloon does not break, two new players (one from each team) attempt the next distance.

Supplies Needed:
- Water Balloons

Instructions to be written on the card:

> WATER BALLOON TOSS
>
> Choose one player from each team. They must successfully toss the balloon from the shortest distance back and forth. If both tosses are successful, two new players move to the next distance. If they are not successful, they can try again, or teams may switch out players to try again.
>
> Once all three distances have been completed, both teams will receive the next clue.

VARIATIONS

AROUND THE WORLD

In this variation, teams "visit" a variety of countries and complete challenges that correlate to those countries.

On Amazon.com you can get flags of different countries for pretty cheap. Think of other ideas on decorations for this variation. You might find some useful ideas from the post I wrote on my blog, SummerCampPro.com, titled Around the World in 80 Days.

Below are some suggested challenges.

UK
- Solve the potions riddle in the book Harry Potter and the Sorcerer's Stone.
- Eat bread with Marmite.

IRISH
- Perform (via a dance instructor or an instructional DVD) an Irish Step Dance routine.
- Eat black pudding (pork meat, fat and blood mixed with barley, suet and oatmeal in a sausage).

GREECE
- Test the teams on their Greek Mythology.
- Run a marathon (okay, maybe just one mile).

ITALY
- Build a structure using spaghetti noodles and marshmallows.
- Teams learn 5 phrases in Italian and are tested on it.

AUSTRALIA
- Throw a boomerang and get it to return.
- Hit a ball pitched by an Aussie with a cricket bat.

NEW ZEALAND
- Find the one ring in Middle Earth, you Hobbit.
- Teach teams to do the Maori Haka (dance) Ka Mate Ka Mate.

JAPAN
- Have teams learn to make sushi rolls.
- Learn how to say the alphabet in Japanese as a team.

CHINA
- Use chopsticks to get 10 jelly beans from one bowl to another.
- Learn the numbers 1-20 in Chinese as a team.

USA
- Re-enact a scene from a favorite Hollywood film. All team members must participate.
- Learn to square dance and perform a whole song while doing what the caller says. You could also change that to line dancing.

MEXICO
- Each team player must kick a soccer ball into a small goal.
- Eat chili-infused grasshoppers.

GENERAL
- Match the countries with their flags.
- Learn to say "Hello" in 10 languages.
- Match the currency to the country.

OFF-SITE

While I have put on a couple of off-site races, I am not the biggest fan. It can be very memorable and a lot of fun, but there are reasons for thinking twice about having your Race off-site. Here are some pros and cons.

Pros
- You have more options for challenges.
- Getting away from camp (or other property) is exciting for kids.
- It can be very memorable.
- If video recording the teams, the footage can make for a great keepsake video.

Cons
- You must find drivers if you are planning to get around via personal cars.
- Additional money for gas or public transportation is needed.
- You'll most likely have to spend money on the challenges.
- It takes significantly more time to set-up.
- You'll most likely have to work with shopkeepers.
- There is the added risk of groups being spread out all over town.
- Parents aren't always on board with going off-site.

Of course, you may not have the facilities available to do an on-site event. This was the reason I planned my first off-site Amazing Race.

Plan on a whole day event. Being off-site means you can go just about anywhere. Therefore, you need more time to travel from one place to the next.

1. Start by writing down as many challenges as you can think to do.
2. Most will require the cooperation of businesses. Contact those businesses and see if they'd be willing to help. You could call, but I've had much more success by personally visiting each business and speaking with the owner or manager. You can, of course, use parks for general challenges, too.
3. Plan out the transportation. Use a variety of transportation modes if possible. Examples include walking, busses, trains and bicycles.
4. Decide on your staffing. There needs to be at least one adult per team. The more supervision the better, though. Ages and number of youths in each group will be factors. You may also need staff or volunteers at each of the challenge areas.
5. Make all the clue cards and include any funds that teams will need for transportation (or just have the adult with them pay for everything).
6. Do a run through of the Race.
7. On the day of, set out the Route Markers and envelopes.

Here is a quick list of some possible challenges that should help your brainstorming session.

1. Visit a magic shop and watch the person at the counter demonstrate three tricks. Your team gets one guess at how each of them are done. If you correctly guess how any one of the tricks are done, you'll get your next clue. If not, you must wait 5 minutes to continue the race.
2. At the Double Tree Hotel, guests get a freshly baked cookie when they check-in. Convince the front desk clerk to give you one of their cookies that are supposed to be for guests only. If you are successful, you will get your next clue. If you are not successful, you must wait 5 minutes before you get your next clue. Oh, and share the cookie with the whole team.
3. At the arcade your team must win 100 tickets to purchase your next clue.
4. Visit a craft shop where the instructor will teach you how to make jewelry.
5. In front of the Italian restaurant your team must sing *That's Amore.* You will be provided with the lyrics. If the manager is satisfied, he will give you your next clue.
6. Go to the toy store and buy the toy listed on this card. Take the toy to the Children's Hospital. Your team will be escorted to a room. Give the toy to that child and spend no less than 10 minutes talking to them. In that time, you must find out their favorite movie, cartoon and food. (This obviously takes some planning. Can also be done at a convalescent home. Instead of a toy, take flowers.)
7. Hit 6 balls at the batting cages.
8. Take turns bowling until your team gets three strikes.
9. At the library, quietly find the book Percy Jackson and the Olympians. Go to page 54, 2nd paragraph, 3rd word. Write it down and give it to the children's librarian for your next clue.
10. Break a board at the local martial arts studio.

11. Collect 10 cans of food from homes in the neighborhood. Take them to the food shelter to donate.
12. Busk for a dollar. Put out a jar or hat. Then sing, act, show your talent. Once you've earned a dollar you will get your next clue. (Teams will need to take a few minutes to build up the courage to do this. Once they start give them 10-15 minutes. If they haven't gotten any tips, have someone you've planted go up and drop a dollar in their jar or hat.)
13. Got to Jamba Juice. Everyone takes a shot of wheat grass.
14. Use the stairs to climb to the roof or top story of the tallest building in the area.
15. Beach clean-up – Go to the beach and fill a trash bag with garbage.
16. Take a tour of a factory. (find a factory that gives tours in your area)
17. There are 20 combination locks on the fence at the high school. On this card is the combination to one of them. Find it and bring the lock with you to your next destination.
18. Here is a picture of a statue that is somewhere in this city. Find the statue for your next clue. You may need to ask the locals for help.
19. Find a machine that flattens pennies and get one done.
20. Recreate the mosaic stone on the table. Your supplies are down the street. You can come back to look at the tile as many times as you need to.

OFF-SITE WITH PHOTOS

This variation is best for teens. It's all about getting the right photos. Unlike a photo scavenger hunt, teams do not get a list of all the photos that need to be taken. Instead, they must complete one photo challenge before being told what the next challenge is.

You could do this via cell phones. When a team takes the photo, they send it to the "race officials" who will then text them their next challenge.

You could also have teams record video.

Below is a list of photo (and video) challenges. You may or may not want to contact businesses ahead of time. One thing I like to do is give a couple of "free passes" to each team. If they find a challenge too difficult, they can pass on it by using one of their "free passes".

1. A photo of your team in front of a fire truck with at least two firemen
2. A photo with the team on a city bus
3. A photo with a fit person in front of a gym (the whole team must be doing muscle poses)
4. A photo of two teammates in the box office of a movie theater
5. A photo of your team on a swing set
6. A photo of the team in Ikea as though they are living in one of the display rooms
7. A photo of a teammate proposing on one knee to a stranger
8. A photo with everyone wearing silly hats
9. A photo of a teammate wrapped like a mummy with toilet paper
10. A photo of the team acting like dogs in a pet store
11. A photo in front of city hall
12. A photo of the team sitting on the floor in a library as one of team members is reading them a children's book
13. A photo of the team doing a human pyramid
14. A photo of a four-legged animal
15. Video of the team singing the Big Mac song in front of McDonalds
16. Video of a stranger singing I'm a Little Teapot
17. Video of the team making 10 free throws at a basketball court
18. Video of the team doing a skit
19. Video of one teammate playing Rock, Paper, Scissors with a police officer
20. Video of the team doing the latest YouTube challenge (a safe one, like the mannequin challenge)

Two other fun things to do:
1. Award bonus points for the best or most creative picture (or video) of each task.
2. Take all the photos and create a slide show.

TIME TRAVEL

In this variation, not only do teams "travel" to different parts of the world, they also "travel" through time. Everything else is the same.

Set up different parts of your property as different time periods and locations, as much as you can.

This can include (not in order):

- The Stone Age
- The Ming Dynasty
- The American Revolution
- The Wild West
- The Viking Age
- The Renaissance
- The Future
- The Forties
- The Sixties
- The Eighties
- Baroque
- The Jazz Age
- The Egyptian New Kingdom period (King Tut)
- The Victorian Era
- Archaic Greece
- The Classic Period of Maya

Here are some example challenges.

- Jurassic Period - Dino Eggs
  Find a dino egg (watermelon) somewhere in the area.
- Greece 300 BC - Olympic Games
  Take turns throwing the nerf javelin until your reach 100 yards collectively.
- Rome 680 BC - Chariot Races
  Build a chariot using the supplies in front of you.
- Scandinavia 800 AD - Viking Ship Race
  Using a cardboard box and duct tape, build a Viking ship that will get you from one end of the pool to the other end without sinking.
- Pirates 1720 AD – Find the Treasure
  Follow the map that leads to the treasure. Collect 5 gold coins and 5 gems.
- Wild West 1875 AD – Gunslinger
  Choose one teammate to shoot the five targets with the Nerf gun. Uh oh, the gun has no ammo. Take turns riding the stick horse around the building to earn ammo. Each "ride" around the building earns you one Nerf dart.

This is just a short list. There are plenty of challenges you could create with all of history to work from. You could also have campers "travel" to the future.

COLOR WAR STYLE

THE AMAZING RACE COLOR WAR

This variation is a combination of The Amazing Race and Color War.

The challenges should be ones you would normally use for a Color War, or even a Camp Olympics.

The Amazing Race is essentially a timed event, so the challenges of this variation will be completed back-to-back.

Also, you will not be running competitions that require teams to play against each other, like a soccer match. Instead, they should be challenges that can be completed individually, like scoring a penalty kick.

Start by dividing the camp into Color teams. Many camps that run Color War divide the camp into two teams. For this Amazing Race variation, I would divide the camp into no less than four teams.

Each competition will have an age group assigned to it. For example, a Lego Tower Build might be for the 7-8 year olds, while the Apache Relay will be for the 15-16 year olds. Once teams get a list of the events, they will assign campers to each one of them. Teams must make sure that all campers are competing in at least one event and no more than two or three events.

Each team will also have a "runner" or multiple runners who will run from one challenge to the next. Teams cannot start a challenge until the runner gets to them.

This is great for an all-day program, but can also be done in a few hours, depending on the competitions and number of campers you have.

You just want to make sure that all the campers get to participate. If there are a few that aren't interested in competing, get them involved in making signs for their teams or being part of the competition set-up crew.

EXAMPLE SCHEDULE

Here's what an all-day Amazing Race (Color War Style) schedule might look like. In this example, the campers range from ages 7-14.

A Day or Two Before the Event
1. Divide the campers into teams.
2. Hand out a list of the challenges along with a sign-up sheet.
3. Have teams assign campers to each of the challenges on the sign-up sheet, and one (or more) to be a runner.
4. Ask campers and staff to wear their color for the Race.

Day of the Event

8am Teams gather for announcements. While staff set-up for the first set of challenges, competitors of the first 6 challenges go to their event spots and get ready. Runners also take their spots.

8:25 One runner from each team lines up at the starting line. The campers who are not competing in this leg can go to the challenge of their choice to cheer on their team.

8:30 The Race begins.

Leg One
- Runners race to the part of camp where groups of three 13-14 year olds are waiting to solve a jigsaw puzzle.
- After solving the jigsaw puzzle, the runner races to the waterfront where three 9-10 year olds and one staff are waiting to canoe across the lake and back.
- When they return the runner races to the basketball court where one 11-12 year old must make 5 free-throws.
- After making the shots the runner races to the dining hall where four 7-8 year olds are waiting to build a Lego structure that must look identical to the example.
- When the Lego structure is complete the runner races to the pool where two 9-10 year olds are waiting. One must swim the length of the pool twice. The other one must dive down to

retrieve 5 pennies, one at a time, from the bottom of the pool but cannot start until the first swimmer is done.
- Once complete, the runner races to the rock-climbing wall where one 13-14 year old is harnessed up waiting to climb to the top.
- After climbing to the top, the runner races to the Pit Stop. When the runner gets there, the teams time stops.

Break Time
- Staff set-up the next set of challenges for the next leg of the race.
- Teams gather together and talk about the event and have a snack.
- Competitors and runners for the next leg take their spots and get ready.
- Just before the Race continues, players not competing in this leg go to the challenge area of their choice to cheer on their team.

Leg Two
You can have all the runners start at the same time and just keep track of the times that teams reach each Pit Stop, or you can have runners start at different times depending on their previous Pit Stop time.

The second leg of the race is like the first leg but with different challenges. The third and fourth legs of the event happen after lunch.

Side note: You can eliminate the "runners" and just have the camper(s) run to the next area after completing their task.

Since the campers know ahead of time what their task will be, there is no need for clue cards or route markers. I know, this variation isn't very Amazing Race-ish, but it does have the element of a race and is a fun way to run a Color War or Camp Olympics.

OTHER VARIATIONS

THE AMAZING RACE OTHER VARIATIONS

An Amazing Race event can have many variations. If you stick with the basic structure of teams racing from one challenge to the next and add in some Detours and Roadblocks, you'll be good.

MOVIE THEMED
Add in Star Wars challenges and have teams "travel" from planet to planet from the Star Wars universe. Or, you could hold a Pixar themed race where each leg is full of challenges from different Pixar movies.

EDUCATION THEMED
With an education themed race all the challenges can be S.T.E.M. related. Teams must complete science experiments, solve computer programming challenges, take on engineering problems and complete math equations.

FAMILY CAMP
Instead of teams of campers, how about families racing against each other. Sounds like a perfect addition to your next family camp.

SUGGESTED ADDITIONS

Over its 30+ seasons The Amazing Race has gone through many changes. They have added and taken away a variety of rules.

Take the Detour, for example. In season 25 they introduced the "Blind Detour" where teams only got the name of each challenge. No other information or description was given before making a choice.

Then in season 26 they introduce "Roulette Detours" where teams spun a roulette wheel to decide which challenge they had to complete.

Roadblock limits have changed many times limiting the number of roadblocks each team member could do.

Fast Forwards used to be available for every leg of the race. Then they changed it to two legs and then to one. This was due to production budgets.

Yields were introduced in season 5 and were replaced by U-Turns in season 12. Then there was the Blind U-Turn, The Double U-Turn and the Automatic U-Turn.

The Intersection has come and gone multiple times. Add in the Express Pass, Salvage Pass, Return Ticket, etc. and you can see that there have been many additions and changes to The Amazing Race over the years.

In this section, I have given you some ideas for additions that will work nicely for a large youth Amazing Race.

TRANSPORTATION HUBS and TOKENS

At the beginning of the race, or leg, you can give each team a set of tokens (or race dollars) to spend on transportation.

Even though teams are not actually having to take transportation like trains and taxis (at least if the Race is done at camp), you can still create areas that you call transportation hubs.

At transportation hubs teams choose what form of transportation they would like to take. Of course, the quicker the transportation, the more expensive it is. That's where the tokens come in.

If teams choose to "purchase" a train ride, they pay 4 tokens and get their next Route Info card which tells them clearly where to go.

If teams choose to "purchase" a taxi ride, they pay 2 tokens, wait 60 seconds, then get their next Route Info card which tells them where to go by way of an easy riddle.

If teams choose to travel by foot, there is no fee. They must wait 2 minutes, and then they get their next Route Info card which tells them where to go by way of a more difficult riddle.

You can, of course, change the token fees and the wait times. You can also give teams the opportunity to use their tokens on food, admission, maps, gear, etc.

USING DICE (WAS THERE A DELAY?)

Another option is to use dice to give the race some additional excitement. In The Amazing Race television program, you may have noticed that sometimes cab drivers get lost, flights get delayed, and teams arrive for their next challenge only to find that the gate is closed until a certain time. There is some luck involved in the Race.

You can add that chance of getting unfortunate circumstances with dice. As each team arrives at a challenge or transportation hub, they must roll the dice to see if their driver got lost, their taxi got a flat or needed gas, a flight got delayed or a team didn't make its connection.

Here is an example:

Roll a 1 = You found some money on the ground (gain two tokens)
Roll a 2 = Your taxi driver needs gas (wait one minute before continuing)
Roll a 3 = Your taxi driver is the best. He's fast and knowledgeable (gain a one minute coupon to be used when needed)
Roll a 4 = Everything ran smooth (no penalty, no advantage)
Roll a 5 = Train is delayed (wait 2 minutes before continuing)
Roll a 6 = Everything ran smooth (no penalty, no advantage)

SWITCH PASSES

Road Blocks are tasks that only one or two team members can perform. Once the team member(s) is chosen, they cannot be switched. These are the normal rules of The Amazing Race. However, because we don't want campers to get too frustrated over choosing the wrong team member, it might be a good idea to include Switch Passes. You can have teams earn the passes, buy them with tokens, or include one in their first envelope.

A Switch Pass allows teams to switch out a team member that is having a difficult time with a Road Block. Each pass can only be used once.

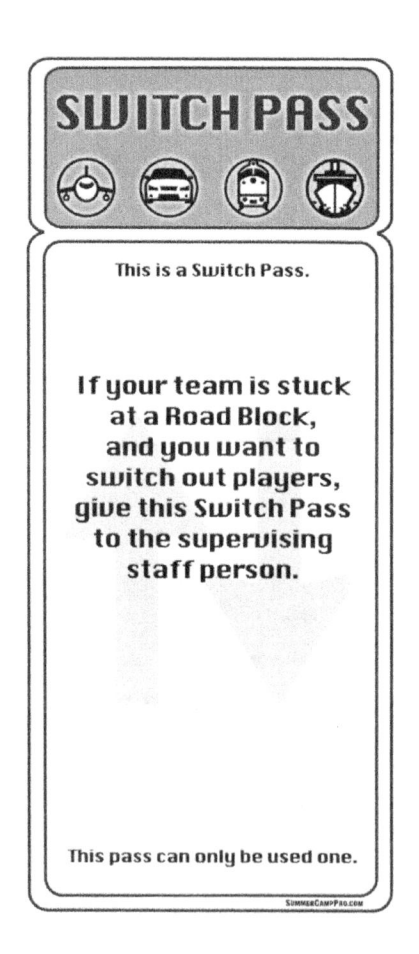

SWITCH PASS

This is a Switch Pass.

If your team is stuck at a Road Block, and you want to switch out players, give this Switch Pass to the supervising staff person.

This pass can only be used one.

SummerCampPro.com

HIDDEN EXPRESS PASS

Somewhere along the path, hidden but not impossible to spot, you could have a Roaming Gnome. You can find Travelocity style Roaming Gnomes on eBay and Amazon. Alternatively, you can buy a regular garden gnome at a gardening center.

If a team finds the gnome, they must turn it in at the next challenge to receive an Express Pass. The Express Pass will allow them to skip a task or will give them a big advantage on one of the tasks.

If you decide to do this, I suggest making the challenge that they skip an easy one that wouldn't have taken much time. This way, the team is excited about having earned the Express Pass, but it doesn't give them such a large time advantage that it ensures they win.

TRAVELING GNOMES

Speaking of gnomes, consider having teams choose a Traveling Gnome after they complete a challenge. Under the gnomes are written numbers.

At the end of the race, have a person pick a number out of a bag. Whichever team has the gnome with that number, they get a fun little prize.

Or, during the race, have them roll a dice. If they roll the same number as the number on their gnome, they get a prize or advantage in the game.

PENALTY FOR NEGATIVE BEHAVIOR OR CHEATING

We don't want any of the teams or campers to cheat, show bad sportsmanship, or show negative behavior in any way. As a deterrent, penalize teams for showing undesired behavior with a five-minute penalty.

Those five minutes can be a good time for their counselor or another staff member to talk to the group about good sportsmanship and fair play. It's also a chance to talk about having a good time and not taking the "competition" of the race so seriously. After all, there is nothing serious at stake. It's all for fun.

ABOUT THE AUTHOR

Curt, a.k.a. Moose, is a youth professional who has worked at a variety of day and overnight summer camps and city recreation departments. As a camp and recreation professional his aim is to serve people who are looking for new camp program ideas.

He started his blog, SummerCampPro.com in 2009 sharing his program ideas and more. Besides writing occasional posts for his blog, he also runs a monthly round table via email. Curt enjoys sharing ideas and collaborating with other camp professionals. The round tables have been a wonderful source of great ideas that he shares through his books.

He also runs a site called Patchwork Marketplace where he and other youth professionals sell their downloadable resources. You can find all his books there in PDF format.

Curt's most recent project is the annual Summer Camp Con, an online conference for camp professionals who cannot afford or find the time to attend an in-person conference. You can find more info at SummerCampCon.com.

A native Californian, Curt travelled full-time in an RV around the US for two years with his dog Max before settling in central Florida.

OTHER BOOKS and RESOURCES
by CURT JACKSON

HOW TO CREATE A LOW COST ESCAPE ROOM:
FOR CAMPS, YOUTH GROUPS AND COMMUNITY CENTERS

HOW TO START AND RUN AN AFTER SCHOOL DRAMA CLASS:
THAT KIDS (AND PARENTS) WILL LOVE!

100 OUTSTANDING SUMMER CAMP PROGRAM IDEAS

101 WAYS TO CREATE AN UNFORGETTABLE CAMP EXPERIENCE

COLOR WAR TIPS, TRICKS AND GREAT IDEAS

100 OUTSTANDING SUMMER CAMP PROGRAM IDEAS

The following can be found at PatchworkMarketplace.com in PDF format.

100 TERRIFIC SUMMER CAMP TEEN/PRE-TEEN PROGRAM IDEAS

101 INCREDIBLE SUMMER CAMP RAINY DAY ACTIVITIES

HOW TO RUN A BEAD REWARD AND RECOGNITION PROGRAM AT SUMMER CAMP

40 WAYS TO SPICE UP YOUR ARCHERY PROGRAM

100 INTERVIEW QUESTIONS FOR POTENTIAL CAMP STAFF

101 PUZZLES FOR LOW COST ESCAPE ROOMS

COLOR WAR TIPS, TRICKS AND GREAT IDEAS

55 FANTASTIC SUMMER CAMP EVENING ACTIVITIES

151 AWESOME SUMMER CAMP NATURE ACTIVITIES

HOW TO CREATE EPIC CAMP-WIDE GAMES:
AND IMPROVE THE CLASSICS USING GAME MECHANICS

CREATING AND RUNNING SCAVENGER AND TREASURE HUNTS

SUPERHEROES THEME BOOK

PIRATE THEME BOOK

STAR WARS THEME BOOK

OLYMPICS THEME BOOK

HOW TO SUCCESSFULLY RUN A GAME SHOW AT CAMP

SUPER STAFF TRAINING BITES

HARRY POTTER THEMED ESCAPE ROOM GAME

TEMPLATES

When I put on my first Race, I spent hours and hours creating just the templates for the cards. I want to give you those templates as a thank you for purchasing this book.

The templates include:

- Editable Challenge Cards
- Editable Route Info Cards
- Editable Road Block Cards
- Editable Detour Cards
- Editable Intersection Cards
- Switch Passes
- Route Markers
- Two Checklists

The editable PDF files allow you to add text to the cards.

Unfortunately, you cannot do anything fancy with the text. If you have something like Photoshop or Adobe Acrobat Pro, then you can make the card text look any way you want.

Go to SummerCampPro.com/AR-Templates.

Made in the USA
Monee, IL
03 April 2020